# The Cat and the Box

By Library For All

Illustrated by Anamika Gautam

Library For All Ltd.

# The cat has a box.

The cat is in the box.

The cat is on the box.

The cat is beside the box.

The cat is in front of the box.

The cat is behind the box.

Where is the cat?

# Cat?

There he is!

## About the contributors

Library For All works with authors and illustrators from around the world to develop diverse, relevant, high-quality books. Visit libraryforall.org for the latest news on writers' workshop events, submission guidelines and other creative opportunities.

# Did you enjoy this book?

We have hundreds more expertly curated original stories to choose from.

We work in partnership with authors, educators, cultural advisors, governments and NGOs to bring the joy of reading to people everywhere.

# Did you know?

We create global impact in these fields by embracing the United Nations Sustainable Development Goals.

library forall.org

# You're reading Level 1

## Learner – Beginner readers

Start your reading journey with short words,
big ideas and plenty of pictures.

## Level 1 – Rising readers

Raise your reading level with more words,
simple sentences and exciting images.

## Level 2 – Eager readers

Enjoy your reading time with familiar words,
but complex sentences.

## Level 3 – Progressing readers

Develop your reading skills with creative stories
and some challenging vocabulary.

## Level 4 – Fluent readers

Step up your reading skills with playful narratives,
new words and fun facts.

## Level 5 – Curious readers

Discover your world through science and stories.

## Level 6 – Adventurous readers

Explore your world through science and stories.

The Cat and the Box

First published 2024

Published by Library For All Ltd
Email: info@libraryforall.org
URL: libraryforall.org

This project was delivered with the support of Edmund Rice Foundation Australia.

**Edmund** Rice
FOUNDATION AUSTRALIA

*Liberating Lives Through Education*

Original illustrations by Anamika Gautam

The Cat and the Box
Library For All
ISBN: 978-1-923207-80-6
SKU04513

www.ingramcontent.com/pod-product-compliance
Lightning Source LLC
Chambersburg PA
CBHW042348040426
42448CB00019B/3458